To my Amelia Marie -

Thanks for loving kitties as much as I do.

You are my greatest treasure.

Published by Orange Hat Publishing 2020
ISBN 978-1-64538-119-8

For information, please contact:

Orange Hat Publishing
www.orangehatpublishing.com
Waukesha, WI

One cold February morning, a curious
kitty walked through the snow.
His daily dose of feline freedom
brought him to a school parking lot.

Growing more curious, he wandered closer.

His keen little ears heard car doors open and close.

Children laughed and ran into the building.

For the first time, the kitty longed for a "furever" home.

A plan pounced his kitty mind.
A teacher spotted him and
stopped to say hello.

Thinking he might need rescuing, she scooped him up and brought him into the warm school.

The little gray kitty hid his face against her coat, frightened by the noisy crowd of children rushing up the hallway.
Had he made a pawful mistake?

They entered the classroom, and to his relief, the children were hushed by a calming "Shhhhhh" sound coming from the teacher.

He sat as still as a statue, minus his twitching tail.

Ms. Catsby's Class

"I was afraid the poor kitty would get hurt in the morning traffic. He will go back outside once the cars clear."

Me, back outside? In the freezing snow? I don't think so!

The clever gray kitty knew it was now urgent for him to reveal his perfect kitty charm. He curled up in the teacher's lap, mustering his loudest purr for the entire class to hear.

Puuurrrr

Katherine whispered, "Ms. Catsby, I hear him purring! He must be such a nice kitty!"

So far, so good.

Leo replied, "Ms. Catsby, you MUST take him home! You just love cats, and he would clearly be the perfect kitty for you!"

The little gray kitty rubbed his head against the teacher's arm, twirling in circles and rubbing again.

Ms. Catsby ran her hand down his velveteen coat and sighed, "I can't bring him home. He may be someone's kitty."

"We could advertise the kitty to the school and neighborhood to see if someone lost him," offered Tabby.

No more kitten around! I need a home!

Ms. Catsby agreed to take the kitty home for safekeeping until the owner was found.

Over the next few days...
The students hung posters.

They advertised in the newspaper.

FOUND
Little gray kitty
Found at Local
Elementary School:
Teacher & Students
Look For His Home

They visited neighbors.

The little gray kitty snuggled
on the couch.

He ate yummy food.

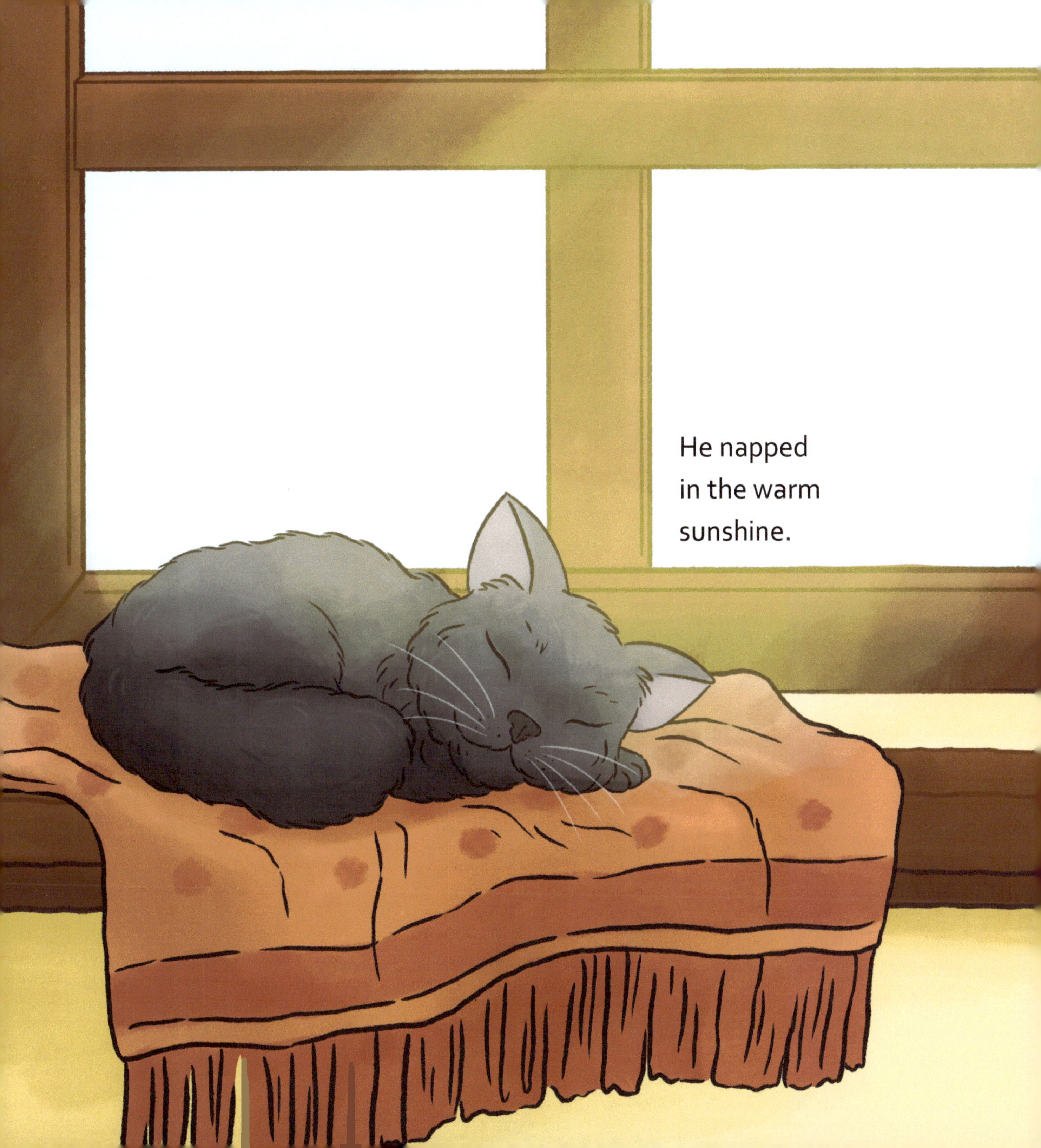

He napped
in the warm
sunshine.

Five days had passed, and he was feeling purrrfectly content at home with Ms. Catsby and her family.

Will she keep me? Will this be my new furever home?

Ms. Catsby loaded up her car, including the kitty, and headed for school.

Her students knew today was the day to find the kitty a home. When she entered the classroom, a hushed silence fell upon her students. The little gray kitty poked his head out of her bag.

What am I doing back at school?

Ms. Catsby's Class

"Class, I'm afraid no one has called about the little gray kitty, but he needs a furever home. So, I would like you to meet Simon P. Catsby...

MY
new
kitty!"

www.ingramcontent.com/pod-product-compliance
Lightning Source LLC
Chambersburg PA
CBHW040740150426
42813CB00064B/2969